Poems

Books by Hermann Hesse

Poems by
Hermann Hesse
Selected and
translated by
James Wright

FARRAR, STRAUS

AND GIROUX

NEW YORK

Farrar, Straus and Giroux
18 West 18th Street, New York 10011

Library of Congress Control Number: 2007934249
ISBN-13: 978-0-374-52641-2
ISBN-10: 0-374-52641-9

10 9 8 7 6 5 4 3 2 1

For Michael di Capua —J.W.

Contents

Translator's Note

Few American readers seem aware that Hesse was a poet.
In the seven-volume German edition of his works, there are
some 480 pages of poems, *Die Gedichte*. Some are very fine,
and it goes without saying that a fine short poem can have
the resonance and depth of an entire good novel. Readers of
Hesse's novels are already aware that they contain many
passages of literal verse. His *Novellen*, that peculiarly German
form which Goethe first mastered and which contains some
of the most profoundly beautiful and illuminating bodies of
feeling in the literature—Keller, Eichendorff, and Storm come
to mind, not to mention the very master of them all, Thomas
Mann—are lyrical in themselves; and one of them, *In the
Pressel Summerhouse* (*Im Presselschen Gartenhaus*), is
itself a story about poets. It deals with the young Mörike's
visit to the aging Hölderlin. It is a story by an artist about an
artist who is visiting another artist, in this case a master,
and it bears some resemblance to Mörike's own prose master-
piece, *Mozart on the Way to Prague* (*Mozart auf der Reise
nach Prag*).

I don't intend here to offer more than an implicit judgment
of Hesse's work. I like his poems very much, or I would not
have tried to translate some of them. But I should say some-
thing about the poet's theme. Both his curious erudition
and his own writings make clear his abiding concern with
art as a way of searching for knowledge. Whether or
not the strange and haunted old man ever learned anything

worth knowing is a matter still open to question. It has been argued by scholars and artists alike. All I wish to do is to offer a selection of Hesse's poems which deal with the single theme of homesickness.

I suppose the word, like love, is simple enough at first glance. If somebody else is in love, love looks charmingly silly. If somebody else is homesick, we chuckle. The poor fellow hasn't grown up. But his struggle, his growth itself, is a serious theme, and Hesse has touched this theme with a traditionally endearing delicacy.

During the recent proliferation of translations which have brought so many of Hesse's works to the attention of American readers, and particularly to the attention of the young, there has been a need to identify him, to describe his limits. Otherwise, he might go the way of a fad, as so many things—and not all of them worthless, either—have a way of doing in America. To my mind, the best criticism of this indispensable kind has been provided by the brilliant American novelist Stephen Koch. He is particularly qualified to warn against the inflation of Hesse. Quite aside from Mr. Koch's own mastery of lyrical prose, and quite aside from his learning, he is himself a young man who has written profoundly in defense of the distressed, assaulted new generation in this country. So, in his penetrating review of Hesse's *Narcissus and Goldmund* (*The New Republic*, July 13, 1968), Mr. Koch describes Hesse's limitations, and thereby, I think, reveals his true powers:

> Like everything else in his work, Hesse's thought is irretrievably adolescent, so that in his chosen role of artist of ideas, he is invariably second-rate, although unlike the other prophets of the New Age, he is never *less* than second-rate. His thought is never cheap, never trashy, but neither is it ever intellectually exalting, the way the professorial, unfashionable Mann so often is. Almost without exception, Hesse's ideas are derivative, school-boyish, traditional to the point of being academic, influenced by all the right people, and boringly correct. [. . .] So it goes, book after book, the Great Ideas chasing the Terrific Experiences home to their all-too-obvious destinations. Flawed though it sometimes is, Hesse's aesthetic sense is different and better than this; *it* does sometimes rise to extraordinary levels, does transform itself into "something else," as the kids say. The final third of *Steppenwolf* is one of the great moments in modern literature, a moment original to the point of being in a class by itself, and one with an importance to future art which is not to be patronized.

I think that Mr. Koch has caught the nature and value of Hesse's art so beautifully in this passage that it remains only to offer yet another few lines, taken from the closing pages of *Steppenwolf*, which I have followed as my guide in selecting and translating some of Hesse's poems. The lines I mean do indeed appear in the final third of *Steppenwolf*. I have abbreviated them; but they provide what I take to be Hesse's best and noblest expression of his artistic theme. In this passage, the girl Hermine is trying to explain to the forty-year-old Harry Haller why his life is nothing, and yet not nothing:

"Time and the world, money and power belong to the small people and the shallow people. To the rest, to the real men belongs nothing. Nothing but death."

"Nothing else?"

"Yes, eternity."

"You mean a name, and fame with posterity?"

"No, Steppenwolf, not fame. Has that any value? And do you think that all true and real men have been famous and known to posterity?"

"No, of course not."

"Then it isn't fame. Fame exists in that sense only for the schoolmasters. No, it isn't fame. It is what I call eternity. The pious call it the kingdom of God. I say to myself: all we who ask too much and have a dimension too many could not contrive to live at all if there were not another air to breathe outside the air of this world, if there were not eternity at the back of time; and this is the kingdom of truth. The music of Mozart belongs there and the poetry of your great poets. The saints, too, belong there, who have worked wonders and suffered martyrdom and given a great example to men. But the image of every true act, the strength of every true feeling, belongs to eternity just as much, even though no one knows of it or sees it or records it or hands it down to posterity. [. . .] Ah, Harry, we have to stumble through so much dirt and humbug before we reach home. And we have no one to guide us. Our only guide is our homesickness."

That is what I think Hesse's poetry is about. He is homesick. But what is home? I do not know the answer, but I cherish Hesse because he at least knew how to ask the question.

A translation of this kind is always a collaboration difficult to identify. But I would like to express my gratitude to Mr. Michael Roloff, who did his best to correct my inaccuracies of translation; to the poet Jerome Mazzaro, a masterful translator whose advice means almost as much as his friendship; and to Mr. and Mrs. Morgan Epes of Buffalo, N.Y., and Mr. and Mrs. Orrin Bly of Old Chatham, N.Y., at whose homes most of these translations were made.

James Wright
February 22, 1970

Poems

Ich weiss, du gehst—

So oft ich spät noch auf der Strasse geh,
Senk ich den Blick und eile voller Angst,
Du könntest plötzlich schweigend vor mir stehn
Und meine Blicke müssten all dein Weh
Und müssten sehn,
Wie du von mir dein totes Glück verlangst.

Ich weiss, du gehst da draussen jede Nacht
Mit scheuem Schritt im schlechten Dirnenputz
Und gehst nach Geld, and siehst so elend aus!
An deinen Schuhen klebt der Schmutz,
Der Wind spielt frech mit deiner Haare Pracht—
Du gehst und gehst, und findst nicht mehr nach Haus.

[1899]

I Know, You Walk—

I walk so often, late, along the streets,
Lower my gaze, and hurry, full of dread,
Suddenly, silently, you still might rise
And I would have to gaze on all your grief
With my own eyes,
While you demand your happiness, that's dead.

I know, you walk beyond me, every night,
With a coy footfall, in a wretched dress
And walk for money, looking miserable!
Your shoes gather God knows what ugly mess,
The wind plays in your hair with lewd delight—
You walk, and walk, and find no home at all.

Über die Felder...

Über den Himmel Wolken ziehn
Über die Felder geht der Wind,
Über die Felder wandert
Meiner Mutter verlorenes Kind.

Über die Strasse Blätter wehn,
Über den Bäumen Vögel schrein—
Irgendwo über den Bergen
Muss meine ferne Heimat sein.

[1902]

Across the Fields . . .

Across the sky, the clouds move,
Across the fields, the wind,
Across the fields the lost child
Of my mother wanders.

Across the street, leaves blow,
Across the trees, birds cry—
Across the mountains, far away,
My home must be.

Elisabeth

Ich soll erzählen,
Die Nacht ist schon spät—
Willst du mich quälen,
Schöne Elisabeth?

Daran ich dichte
Und du dazu,
Meine Liebesgeschichte
Ist dieser Abend und du.

Du musst nicht stören,
Die Reime verwehn.
Bald wirst du sie hören,
Hören und nicht verstehn.

[1902]

Elizabeth

I should tell you a story,
The night is already so late—
Do you want to torment me,
Lovely Elizabeth?

I write poems about that,
Just as you do;
And the entire history of my love
Is you and this evening.

You mustn't be troublesome,
And blow these poems away.
Soon you will listen to them,
Listen, and not understand.

Ravenna (1)

Ich bin auch in Ravenna gewesen.
Ist eine kleine tote Stadt,
Die Kirchen und viel Ruinen hat,
Man kann davon in den Büchern lesen.

Du gehst hindurch und schaust dich um,
Die Strassen sind so trüb und nass
Und sind so tausendjährig stumm
Und überall wächst Moos und Gras.

Das ist wie alte Lieder sind—
Man hört sie an und keiner lacht
Und jeder lauscht und jeder sinnt
Hernach daran bis in die Nacht.

[1902]

Ravenna (1)

I, too, have been in Ravenna.
It is a little dead city
That has churches and a good many ruins.
You can read about it in books.

You walk back through it and look around you:
The streets are so muddy and damp, and so
Dumbstruck for a thousand years,
And moss and grass, everywhere.

That is what old songs are like—
You listen to them, and nobody laughs
And everybody draws back into
His own time till night falls into him.

Ravenna (2)

Die Frauen von Ravenna tragen
Mit tiefem Blick und zarter Geste
In sich ein Wissen von den Tagen
Der alten Stadt und ihrer Feste.

Die Frauen von Ravenna weinen
Wie stille Kinder: tief und leise.
Und wenn sie lachen, will es scheinen
Zu trübem Text die helle Weise.

Die Frauen von Ravenna beten
Wie Kinder: sanft und voll Genügen.
Sie können Liebesworte reden
Und selbst nicht wissen, dass sie lügen.

Die Frauen von Ravenna küssen
Seltsam und tief und hingegeben.
Und ihnen allen ist vom Leben
Nichts kund, als dass wir sterben müssen.

[1902]

Ravenna (2)

The women of Ravenna,
With their deep gazes and affectionate gestures,
Carry a knowledge of the days
Of the old city, their festivals.

The women of Ravenna
Weep like children who won't tell you: deep, light.
And when they laugh, a glittering song
Rises in the sludge of the text.

The women of Ravenna pray
Like children: gentle, fully contented.
They can speak love's words without even knowing
Themselves they are lying.

The women of Ravenna kiss
Rarely and deep, they kiss back.
And all they know about life is that
We all have to die.

Einsame Nacht

Die ihr meine Brüder seid,
Arme Menschen nah und ferne,
Die ihr im Bezirk der Sterne
Tröstung träumet eurem Leid,
Die ihr wortelos gefaltet
In die blass gestirnte Nacht
Schmale Dulderhände haltet,
Die ihr leidet, die ihr wacht,
Arme, irrende Gemeinde,
Schiffer ohne Stern und Glück—
Fremde, dennoch mir Vereinte,
Gebt mir meinen Gruss zurück!

[1902]

Lonesome Night

You brothers, who are mine,
Poor people, near and far,
Longing for every star,
Dream of relief from pain,
You, stumbling dumb
At night, as pale stars break,
Lift your thin hands for some
Hope, and suffer, and wake,
Poor muddling commonplace,
You sailors who must live
Unstarred by hopelessness,
We share a single face.
Give me my welcome back.

Mückenschwarm

Viel tausend glänzende Punkte
Drängen sich gierig in Fieberwonnen
Zu zitternden Kreisen zusammen.
Verschwenderisch prassend
Eine eilig entgleitende Stunde lang
Rasen sie wild mit gellem Geräusch
In zuckender Lust dem Tod entgegen.

Untergegangene Reiche,
Deren goldbeladene Throne plötzlich und spurlos
In Nacht und Sage zerstoben,
Haben nie so wilde Tänze gekannt.

[1911]

A Swarm of Gnats

Many thousand glittering motes
Crowd forward greedily together
In trembling circles.
Extravagantly carousing away
For a whole hour rapidly vanishing,
They rave, delirious, a shrill whir,
Shivering with joy against death.

Whole kingdoms, sunk into ruin,
Whose thrones, heavy with gold, instantly scattered
Into night and legend, without leaving a trace,
Have never known of so fierce a dancing.

Der Dichter

Nur mir dem Einsamen
Scheinen des Nachts die unendlichen Sterne,
Rauscht der steinerne Brunnen sein Zauberlied,
Mir allein, mir dem Einsamen
Ziehen die farbigen Schatten
Wandernder Wolken Träumen gleich übers Gefild.
Nicht Haus noch Acker ist,
Nicht Wald noch Jagd noch Gewerb mir gegeben,
Mein ist nur, was keinem gehört,
Mein ist stürzender Bach hinterm Waldesschleier,
Mein das furchtbare Meer,
Mein der spielenden Kinder Vogelgeschwirre,
Träne und Lied einsam Verliebter am Abend.
Mein auch sind die Tempel der Götter, mein ist
Der Vergangenheit ehrwürdiger Hain.
Und nicht minder der Zukunft
Lichtes Himmelsgewölbe ist meine Heimat:
Oft in Flügen der Sehnsucht stürmt meine Seele empor,
Seliger Menschheit Zukunft zu schauen,
Liebe, Gesetz besiegend, Liebe von Volk zu Volk.
Alle find ich sie wieder, edel verwandelt:
Landmann, König, Händler, emsiges Schiffervolk,
Hirt und Gärtner, sie alle
Feiern dankbar der Zukunft Weltfest.
Einzig der Dichter fehlt,

The Poet

Only on me, the lonely one,
The unending stars of the night shine,
The stone fountain whispers its magic song,
To me alone, to me the lonely one
The colorful shadows of the wandering clouds
Move like dreams over the open countryside.
Neither house nor farmland,
Neither forest nor hunting privilege is given to me,
What is mine belongs to no one,
The plunging brook behind the veil of the woods,
The frightening sea,
The bird whir of children at play,
The weeping and singing, lonely in the evening, of a man
    secretly in love.
The temples of the gods are mine also, and mine
The aristocratic groves of the past.
And no less, the luminous
Vault of heaven in the future is my home:
Often in full flight of longing my soul storms upward,
To gaze on the future of blessed men,
Love, overcoming the law, love from people to people.
I find them all again, nobly transformed:
Farmer, king, tradesman, busy sailors,
Shepherd and gardener, all of them
Gratefully celebrate the festival of the future world.
Only the poet is missing,

Er, der vereinsamt Schauende,
Er, der Menschensehnsucht Träger und bleiches Bild,
Dessen die Zukunft, dessen die Welterfüllung
Nicht mehr bedarf. Es welken
Viele Kränze an seinem Grabe,
Aber verschollen ist sein Gedächtnis.

[1911]

The lonely one who looks on,
The bearer of human longing, the pale image
Of whom the future, the fulfillment of the world
Has no further need. Many garlands
Wilt on his grave,
But no one remembers him.

Berge in der Nacht

Der See ist erloschen,
Schwarz schläft das Ried,
Im Traume flüsternd.
Ungeheuer ins Land gedehnt
Drohen die hingestreckten Berge.
Sie ruhen nicht.
Sie atmen tief, und sie halten
Einer den andern an sich gedrückt.
Tief atmend,
Mit dumpfen Kräften beladen,
Unerlöst in verzehrender Leidenschaft.

[1911]

Mountains at Night

The lake has died down,
The reed, black in its sleep,
Whispers in a dream.
Expanding immensely into the countryside,
The mountains loom, outspread.
They are not resting.
They breathe deeply, and hold themselves,
Pressed tightly, to one another.
Deeply breathing,
Laden with mute forces,
Caught in a wasting passion.

Bei Nacht

Nachts, wenn das Meer mich wiegt
Und bleicher Sternenglanz
Auf seinen weiten Wellen liegt,
Dann löse ich mich ganz
Von allem Tun und aller Liebe los
Und stehe still und atme bloss
Allein, allein vom Meer gewiegt,
Das still und kalt mit tausend Lichtern liegt.
Dann muss ich meiner Freunde denken
Und meinen Blick in ihre Blicke senken,
Und frage jeden still allein:
"Bist du noch mein?
Ist dir mein Leid ein Leid, mein Tod ein Tod?
Fühlst du von meiner Liebe, meiner Not
Nur einen Hauch, nur einen Widerhall?"

Und ruhig blickt und schweigt das Meer
Und lächelt: Nein.
Und nirgendwo kommt Gruss und Antwort her.

[1911]

At Night on the High Seas

(from an Asian journey: Malayan Archipelago)

At night, when the sea cradles me
And the pale star gleam
Lies down on its broad waves,
Then I free myself wholly
From all activity and all the love
And stand silent and breathe purely,
Alone, alone cradled by the sea
That lies there, cold and silent, with a thousand lights.
Then I have to think of my friends
And my gaze sinks into their gazes
And I ask each one, silent, alone:
"Are you still mine?
Is my sorrow a sorrow to you, my death a death?
Do you feel from my love, my grief,
Just a breath, just an echo?"

And the sea peacefully gazes back, silent,
And smiles: no.
And no greeting and no answer comes from anywhere.

An eine chinesische Sängerin

Auf dem stillen Flusse sind wir am Abend gefahren,
Rosig stand und beglänzt der Akazienbaum,
Rosig strahlten die Wolken. Ich aber sah sie kaum,
Sah nur die Pflaumenblüte in deinen Haaren.

Lächelnd sassest du vorn im geschmückten Boote,
Hieltest die Laute in der geübten Hand,
Sangest das Lied vom heiligen Vaterland,
Während in deinen Augen die Jugend lohte.

Schweigend stand ich am Mast und wünschte mir, ohne
    Ende
Dieser glühenden Augen Sklave zu sein,
Ewig dem Liede zu lauschen in seliger Pein
Und dem beglückenden Spiel deiner blumenhaft zarten
    Hände.

[1915]

To a Chinese Girl Singing

We traveled down the still river in the evening,
The acacia stood in the color of rose, casting its light,
The clouds cast down the rose light. But I scarcely saw
    them,
All I saw were the plum blossoms in your hair.

You sat smiling in the bow of the garlanded boat,
Held the lute in your skillful hand,
Sang the song, that holy country of your own,
While your eyes promised fire, and you were so young.

Without saying anything, I stood at the mast, and what I
    wanted,
For myself, was to give in to those gleaming eyes, over and
    over,
To listen to the song forever in blessed pain,
To the song that could make me happy, tangled in your
    delicate hands.

Abschied vom Urwald

Auf meiner Kiste sitz ich am Strand,
Drunten am Dampfer schreien
Inder, Chinesen, Malaien,
Lachen laut und handeln mit Flittertand.

Hinter mir liegen fiebernde Nächte und Tage
Glühenden Lebens, die ich schon jetzt,
Da noch der Urwaldstrom meine Sohlen netzt,
Sorgsam wie Schätze im tiefsten Gedächtnis trage.

Viele Länder und Städte weiss ich noch warten,
Aber niemals wohl wird der Wälder Nacht,
Wird der wilde gärende Urweltgarten
Wieder mich locken und schrecken mit seiner Pracht.

Hier in dieser unendlichen leuchtenden Wildnis
War ich weiter als je entrückt von der Menschenwelt—
O und niemals sah ich so nah und unverstellt
Meiner eigenen Seele gespiegeltes Bildnis.

[1915]

Departure from the Jungle

With my suitcase, I sit on the beach;
Below me, on the steamer, Indians,
Chinese, Malayans are shouting,
Laughing loudly and trading their knickknacks.

Behind me, feverish nights, and days
Of glowing life, that even now I carry
Carefully as treasures in my deepest thoughts,
As though I still wet my feet in the jungle stream.

I know many countries and cities are still waiting,
But never again will the night of the forests,
The wild fermenting garden of the earliest world
Lure me in, and horrify me with its magnificence.

Here in this endless and gleaming wilderness
I was removed farther than ever from the world of men—
And I never saw so close and so clearly
The image in the mirror of my own soul.

Böse Zeit

Nun sind wir still
Und singen keine Lieder mehr,
Der Schritt wird schwer;
Das ist die Nacht, die kommen will.

Gib mir die Hand,
Vielleicht ist unser Weg noch weit.
Es schneit, es schneit!
Hart ist der Winter im fremden Land.

Wo ist die Zeit,
Da uns ein Licht, ein Herd gebrannt?
Gib mir die Hand!
Vielleicht ist unser Weg noch weit.

[1911]

Evil Time

Now we are silent
And sing no songs any more,
Our pace grows heavy;
This is the night, that was bound to come.

Give me your hand,
Perhaps we still have a long way to go.
It's snowing, it's snowing.
Winter is a hard thing in a strange country.

Where is the time
When a light, a hearth burned for us?
Give me your hand!
Perhaps we still have a long way to go.

Auf Wanderung

(DEM ANDENKEN KNULPS)

Sei nicht traurig, bald ist es Nacht,
Da sehn wir über dem bleichen Land
Den kühlen Mond, wie er heimlich lacht,
Und ruhen Hand in Hand.

Sei nicht traurig, bald kommt die Zeit,
Da haben wir Ruh. Unsre Kreuzlein stehen
Am hellen Strassenrande zu zweit,
Und es regnet und schneit,
Und die Winde kommen und gehen.

[1911]

On a Journey

(IN MEMORY OF KNULP)

Don't be downcast, soon the night will come,
When we can see the cool moon laughing in secret
Over the faint countryside,
And we rest, hand in hand.

Don't be downcast, the time will soon come
When we can have rest. Our small crosses will stand
On the bright edge of the road together,
And rain fall, and snow fall,
And the winds come and go.

Wohl lieb ich die finstre Nacht

Wohl lieb ich die finstre Nacht;
Oft aber, wenn sie also bleich
Und düster wie aus Schmerzen lacht,
Graut mir vor ihrem argen Reich
Und ich sehne mich, die Sonne zu schauen
Und lichterfüllte Wolken im Blauen,
Um warm in glänzenden Tagesräumen
Von der Nacht zu träumen.

[1911]

Night

I like the dark night well enough;
But sometimes, when it turns bleak
And peaked, as my suffering laughs at me,
Its dreadful kingdom horrifies me,
And I wish to God I could take one look at the sunlight
And the blue of heaven brought back to light by its clouds,
And I want to lie down warm in the wide spaces of the
    day.
Then I can dream of the night.

Schicksal

Wir sind in Zorn und Unverstand
Wie Kinder tun, geschieden
Und haben uns gemieden,
Von blöder Scham gebannt.

Die Jahre gingen drüber her
Mit Reuen und mit Warten.
In unserm Jugendgarten
Führt keine Strasse mehr.

[1911]

Destiny

In our fury and muddle
We act like children, cut off,
Fled from ourselves,
Bound by silly shame.

The years clump past
In their agony, waiting.
Not a single path leads back
To the garden of our youth.

Ode an Hölderlin

Freund meiner Jugend, zu dir kehr ich voll Dankbarkeit
Manchen Abend zurück, wenn im Fliedergebüsch
Des entschlummerten Gartens
Nur der rauschende Brunnen noch tönt.

Keiner kennt dich, o Freund; weit hat die neuere Zeit
Sich von Griechenlands stillen Zaubern entfernt,
Ohne Gebet und entgöttert
Wandelt nüchtern das Volk im Staub.

Aber der heimlichen Schar innig Versunkener,
Denen der Gott die Seele mit Sehnsucht schlug,
Ihr erklingen die Lieder
Deiner göttlichen Harfe noch heut.

Sehnlich wenden wir uns, vom Tag Ermüdete,
Der ambrosischen Nacht deiner Gesänge zu,
Deren wehender Fittich
Uns beschattet mit goldenem Traum.

Ach, und glühender brennt, wenn dein Lied uns entzückt,
Schmerzlicher brennt nach der Vorzeit seligem Land,
Nach den Tempeln der Griechen
Unser ewiges Heimweh auf.

[1911]

Ode to Hölderlin

Friend of my young manhood, on many an evening
I return gratefully to you, when in the elder bushes
Of the garden fallen asleep
Only the rustling fountains still make a sound.

Nobody knows you, my friend; this new age has driven
Far away from the silent magic of Greece.
Without prayer, and cheated out of gods,
People stroll reasonably in the dust.

But to the secret gathering who sink in their inner lives,
Whose souls God has stricken with longing,
The heavenly strings of your songs
Are ringing, even today.

We turn passionately, exhausted by day,
To the ambrosia, the night of your music,
Whose fanning wing casts us into
A shadow of golden dream.

Yes, and luminously, when your song delights us,
Sorrowfully burning for the blessed land of the past,
For the temples of the Greeks,
Our homesickness lasts forever.

Die Kindheit

Du bist, mein fernes Tal,
Verzaubert und versunken.
Oft hast du mir in Not und Qual
Empor aus deinem Schattenland gewunken
Und deine Märchenaugen aufgetan,
Dass ich entzückt in kurzem Wahn
Mich ganz zu dir zurück verlor.

O dunkles Tor,
O dunkle Todesstunde,
Komm du heran, dass ich gesunde
Und dass aus dieses Lebens Leere
Ich heim zu meinen Träumen kehre!

[1915]

Childhood

My farthest valley, you are
Bewitched and vanished.
Many times, in my grief and agony,
You have beckoned upward to me from your country of
    shadows
And opened your legendary eyes
Till I, lost in a quick illusion,
Lost myself back to you wholly.

O dark gate,
O dark hour of death,
Come forth,
So I can recover from this life's emptiness
And go home to my own dreams.

Im Grase liegend

Ist dies nun alles, Blumengaukelspiel
Und Farbenflaum der lichten Sommerwiese,
Zartblau gespannter Himmel, Bienensang,
Ist dies nun alles eines Gottes
Stöhnender Traum,
Schrei unbewusster Kräfte nach Erlösung?
Des Berges ferne Linie,
Die schön und kühn im Blauen ruht,
Ist denn auch sie nur Krampf,
Nur wilde Spannung gärender Natur,
Nur Weh, nur Qual, nur sinnlos tastende,
Nie rastende, nie selige Bewegung?
Ach nein! Verlass mich du, unholder Traum
Vom Leid der Welt!
Dich wiegt ein Mückentanz im Abendglast,
Dich wiegt ein Vogelruf,
Ein Windhauch auf, der mir die Stirn
Mit Schmeicheln kühlt.
Verlass mich du, uraltes Menschenweh!
Mag alles Qual,
Mag alles Leid und Schatten sein—
Doch diese eine süsse Sonnenstunde nicht,
Und nicht der Duft vom roten Klee,
Und nicht das tiefe, zarte Wohlgefühl
In meiner Seele.

[1915]

Lying in Grass

Is this everything now, the quick delusions of flowers,
And the down colors of the bright summer meadow,
The soft blue spread of heaven, the bees' song,
Is this everything only a god's
Groaning dream,
The cry of unconscious powers for deliverance?
The distant line of the mountain,
That beautifully and courageously rests in the blue,
Is this too only a convulsion,
Only the wild strain of fermenting nature,
Only grief, only agony, only meaningless fumbling,
Never resting, never a blessed movement?
No! Leave me alone, you impure dream
Of the world in suffering!
The dance of tiny insects cradles you in an evening
    radiance,
The bird's cry cradles you,
A breath of wind cools my forehead
With consolation.
Leave me alone, you unendurably old human grief!
Let it all be pain,
Let it all be suffering, let it be wretched—
But not this one sweet hour in the summer,
And not the fragrance of the red clover,
And not the deep tender pleasure
In my soul.

Wie sind die Tage...

Wie sind die Tage schwer!
An keinem Feuer kann ich erwarmen,
Keine Sonne lacht mir mehr,
Ist alles leer,
Ist alles kalt und ohne Erbarmen,
Und auch die lieben klaren
Sterne schauen mich trostlos an,
Seit ich im Herzen erfahren,
Dass Liebe sterben kann.

[1911]

How Heavy the Days . . .

How heavy the days are.
There's not a fire that can warm me,
Not a sun to laugh with me,
Everything bare,
Everything cold and merciless,
And even the beloved, clear
Stars look desolately down,
Since I learned in my heart that
Love can die.

In einer Sammlung ägyptischer Bildwerke

Aus den Edelsteinaugen
Blicket ihr still und ewig
Über uns späte Brüder hinweg.
Nicht Liebe scheint noch Verlangen
Euren schimmernd glatten Zügen bekannt.
Königlich und den Gestirnen verschwistert
Seid ihr Unbegreiflichen einst
Zwischen Tempeln geschritten,
Heiligkeit weht wie ein ferner Götterduft
Heut noch um eure Stirnen,
Würde um eure Knie;
Eure Schönheit atmet gelassen,
Ihre Heimat ist Ewigkeit.

Aber wir, eure jüngeren Brüder,
Taumeln gottlos ein irres Leben entlang,
Allen Qualen der Leidenschaft,
Jeder brennenden Sehnsucht
Steht unsre zitternde Seele gierig geöffnet.
Unser Ziel ist der Tod,
Unser Glaube Vergänglichkeit,
Keiner Zeitenferne
Trotzt unser flehendes Bildnis.
Dennoch tragen auch wir
Heimlicher Seelenverwandtschaft Merkmal
In die Seele gebrannt,

In a Collection
of Egyptian Sculptures

Out of jeweled eyes
Silent and eternal, you gaze away
Over us late brothers.
Neither love nor longing appears to be known among
Your smooth gleaming procession.
Once, inconceivable, you walked, majestic
Brothers and sisters of constellations,
Among the temples.
Even today, holiness like the distant fragrance of gods
Drifts round your brows,
Dignity round your knees:
Your beauty breathes calmly,
Your home is eternity.

But we, your younger brothers,
Stagger godless through a confusing life,
Our trembling souls stand eagerly, opened
To all the sufferings of passion,
To every burning desire.
Our goal is death,
Our belief a belief in what perishes,
No great distance of time defies
Our fleeting faces.
Nevertheless, we also
Bear, burned into our very souls,
The sign of a secret affinity to the spirit,

Ahnen Götter und fühlen vor euch,
Schweigende Bilder der Vorzeit,
Furchtlose Liebe. Denn sehet,
Uns ist kein Wesen verhasst, auch der Tod nicht,
Leiden und Sterben
Schreckt unsre Seele nicht,
Weil wir tiefer zu lieben gelernt!
Unser Herz ist des Vogels,
Ist des Meeres und Walds, und wir nennen
Sklaven und Elende Brüder,
Nennen mit Liebesnamen noch Tier und Stein.
So auch werden die Bildnisse
Unsres vegänglichen Seins
Nicht im harten Steine uns überdauern;
Lächelnd werden sie schwinden
Und im flüchtigen Sonnenstaub
Jeder Stunde zu neuen Freuden und Qualen
Ungeduldig und ewig auferstehn.

[1915]

46

We have a foreboding of gods, a feeling for you,
Images of the silent past,
A fearless love. Look:
We hate nothing that exists, not even death,
Suffering and dying
Does not horrify our souls,
As long as we learn more deeply to love.
Our heart is the bird's heart,
And it belongs to the sea and the forest, and we name
Slaves and wretches our brothers,
We still name with loving names both animal and stone.
So also the images
Of our perishing lives will not survive us
In hard stone:
They will vanish smiling,
And in the flickering dust of sunlight
Every hour to new joys and unhappiness,
Impatient, eternal, they will rise.

Ohne dich

Mein Kissen schaut mich an zur Nacht
Leer wie ein Totenstein;
So bitter hatt ich's nie gedacht,
Allein zu sein
Und nicht in deinem Haar gebettet sein!

Ich lieg allein im stillen Haus,
Die Ampel ausgetan,
Und strecke sacht die Hände aus,
Die deinen zu umfahn,
Und dränge leis den heissen Mund
Nach dir und küss mich matt und wund—
Und plötzlich bin ich aufgewacht
Und ringsum schweigt die kalte Nacht,
Der Stern im Fenster schimmert klar—
O du, wo ist dein blondes Haar,
Wo ist dein süsser Mund?

Nun trink ich Weh in jeder Lust
Und Gift in jedem Wein;
So bitter hatt ich's nie gewusst,
Allein zu sein,
Allein und ohne dich zu sein!

[1915]

Without You

My pillow gazes upon me at night
Empty as a gravestone;
I never thought it would be so bitter
To be alone,
Not to lie down asleep in your hair.

I lie alone in a silent house,
The hanging lamp darkened,
And gently stretch out my hands
To gather in yours,
And softly press my warm mouth
Toward you, and kiss myself, exhausted and weak—
Then suddenly I'm awake
And all around me the cold night grows still.
The star in the window shines clearly—
Where is your blond hair,
Where your sweet mouth?

Now I drink pain in every delight
And poison in every wine;
I never knew it would be so bitter
To be alone,
Alone, without you.

Die ersten Blumen

Neben dem Bach
Den roten Weiden nach
Haben in diesen Tagen
Gelbe Blumen viel
Ihre Goldaugen aufgeschlagen.
Und mir, der längst aus der Unschuld fiel,
Rührt sich Erinnerung im Grunde
An meines Lebens goldene Morgenstunde
Und sieht mich hell aus Blumenaugen an.
Ich wollte Blumen brechen gehn;
Nun lass ich sie alle stehn
Und gehe heim, ein alter Mann.

[1915]

The First Flowers

Beside the brook
Toward the willows,
During these days
So many yellow flowers have opened
Their eyes into gold.
I have long since lost my innocence, yet a memory
Touches my depth, the golden hours of morning, and gazes
Brilliantly upon me out of the eyes of flowers.
I was going to pick flowers;
Now I leave them all standing
And walk home, an old man.

Frühlingstag

Wind im Gesträuch und Vogelpfiff
Und hoch im höchsten süssen Blau
Ein stilles, stolzes Wolkenschiff . . .
Ich träume von einer blonden Frau,
Ich träume von meiner Jugendzeit,
Der hohe Himmel blau und weit
Ist meiner Sehnsucht Wiege,
Darin ich stillgesinnt
Und selig warm
Mit leisem Summen liege,
So wie in seiner Mutter Arm
Ein Kind.

[1915]

Spring Day

Wind in bushes and bird piping
And high in the highest fresh blue
A haughty cloud ship, becalmed . . .
I dream of a blond woman,
I dream of my youth,
The high heaven blue and outspread
Is the cradle of my longing
Where I choose to lie calm
And blessedly warm
With the soft humming,
Just like a child held
On his mother's arm.

Feierliche Abendmusik

Allegro

Gewölk zerreisst; vom glühenden Himmel her
Irrt taumelndes Licht über geblendete Täler.
Mitgeweht vom föhnigen Sturm
Flieh ich mit unermüdetem Schritt
Durch ein bewölktes Leben.
Oh, dass nur immer für Augenblicke
Zwischen mir und dem ewigen Licht
Gütig ein Sturm die grauen Nebel verweht!
Fremdes Land umgibt mich,
Losgerissen treibt von der Heimat fern
Mich des Schicksals mächtige Woge umher.
Jage die Wolken, Föhn,
Reisse die Schleier hinweg,
Dass mir Licht auf die zweifelnden Pfade falle!

Andante

Immer wieder tröstlich
Und immer neu in ewiger Schöpfung Glanz
Lacht mir die Welt ins Auge,
Lebt und regt sich in tausend atmenden Formen,
Flattert Falter im sonnigen Wind,
Segelt Schwalbe in seliger Bläue,

Holiday Music in the Evening

Allegro

The cloudbank breaks up; down from the luminous heaven
Giddy light fumbles across the bedazzled valleys.
Blown by the storm of south wind
I flutter along, unwearied,
Through an overcast life.
Oh, if only for a moment
Between me and the light that lasts forever
A storm would be kind enough to shatter the fog.
Strange country surrounds me,
Overwhelming breakers drive me, torn loose
Far away, from my home to this place.
South wind, hunt down the clouds,
Tear the veil away,
So light can fall on me among the confusing paths.

Andante

Again, every time, comforting
And, every time, new in the gleam of endless creation,
The world laughs in my eyes,
Comes alive and stirs into a thousand breathing forms,
Butterflies tumble in the wind streaming with sunlight,
Swallows sail into the blessing, the blue light,

Strömt Meerflut am felsigen Strand.
Immer wieder ist Stern und Baum,
Ist mir Wolke und Vogel nahe verwandt,
Grüsst mich als Bruder der Fels,
Ruft mir freundschaftlich das unendliche Meer.
Unverstanden führt mich mein Weg
Einer blau verlorenen Ferne zu,
Nirgend ist Sinn, nirgend ist sicheres Ziel—
Dennoch redet mir jeder Waldbach,
Jede summende Fliege von tiefem Gesetz,
Heiliger Ordnung,
Deren Himmelsgewölb' auch mich überspannt,
Deren heimliches Tönen
Wie im Gang der Gestirne
So auch in meines Herzens Taktschlag klingt.

Adagio

Traum gibt, was Tag verschloss;
Nachts, wenn der Wille erliegt,
Streben befreite Kräfte empor,
Göttlicher Ahnung folgend.
Wald rauscht und Strom, und durch der regen Seele
Nachtblauen Himmel Wetterleuchten weht.

Sea waves stream on the beach rocks.
Again, every time, star and tree,
Cloud and bird, my close kindred;
The stone greets me as brother,
The unending sea calls me, friendly.
My road, that I do not understand, leads me
Toward a blue, lost distance,
Nowhere a meaning, nowhere a definite goal—
Nevertheless, every forest brook speaks to me,
And every humming fly, of a deep law,
A right way that is holy,
Whose firmament spreads out above me also,
Whose secret tones,
As in the pace of the stars,
Beat time in my heart as well.

Adagio

A dream gives what the day wore out;
At night, when the conscious will surrenders,
Some powers, set free, reach upward,
Sensing something godly, and following.
The woods rustle, and the stream, and through the night-
    blue sky
Of the quick soul, the summer lightning blows.

In mir und ausser mir
Ist ungeschieden, Welt und ich ist eins.
Wolke weht durch mein Herz,
Wald träumt meinen Traum,
Haus und Birnbaum erzählt mir
Die vergessene Sage gemeinsamer Kindheit.
Ströme hallen und Schluchten schatten in mir,
Mond ist und bleicher Stern mein vertrauter Gespiele.
Aber die milde Nacht,
Die sich über mich mit sanftem Gewölke neigt,
Hat meiner Mutter Gesicht,
Küsst mich lächelnd in unerschöpflicher Liebe,
Schüttelt träumerisch wie in alter Zeit
Ihr geliebtes Haupt, und ihr Haar
Wallt durch die Welt, und es zittern
Blass aufzuckend darin die tausend Sterne.

[1 9 1 1]

The world and my self, everything
Within and without me, grows into one.
Clouds drift through my heart,
Woods dream my dream,
House and pear tree tell me
The forgotten story of common childhood.
Streams resound and gorges cast shadows in me,
The moon, and the faint star, my close friends.
But the mild night,
That bows with its gentle clouds above me,
Has my mother's face,
Kisses me, smiling, with inexhaustible love,
Shakes her head dreamily
As she used to do, and her hair
Waves through the world, and within it
The thousand stars, shuddering, turn pale.

Denken an den Freund
bei Nacht

(SEPTEMBER 1914)

Früh kommt in diesem bösen Jahr der Herbst . . .
Ich geh bei Nacht im Feld, allein, den Wind am Hut,
Der Regen klirrt . . . Und du? Und du, mein Freund?

Du stehst—vielleicht—und siehst den Sichelmond
Im kleinen Bogen über Wälder gehn
Und Biwakfeuer rot im schwarzen Tal.
Du liegst—vielleicht—im Feld auf Stroh und schläfst
Und über Stirn und Waffenrock fällt kalt der Tau.

Kann sein, du bist zu Pferde diese Nacht,
Vorposten, spähend unterwegs, Revolver in der Faust,
Flüsternd und lächelnd mit dem müden Gaul.
Vielleicht—ich denk mir's so—bist du die Nacht
In einem fremden Schloss und Park zu Gast
Und schreibst bei Kerzenlicht an einem Brief,
Und tippst am Flügel im Vorübergehn
Auf klingende Tasten . . .
                                    —Und vielleicht
Bist du schon still, schon tot, und deinen lieben
Ernsthaften Augen scheint der Tag nicht mehr,
Und deine liebe, braune Hand hängt welk,
Und deine weisse Stirne klafft—o hätt ich,

Thinking of a Friend
at Night

(SEPTEMBER 1914)

In this evil year, autumn comes early . . .
I walk by night in the field, alone, the rain clatters,
The wind on my hat . . . And you? And you, my friend?

You are standing—maybe—and seeing the sickle moon
Move in a small arc over the forests
And bivouac fire, red in the black valley.
You are lying—maybe—in a straw field and sleeping
And dew falls cold on your forehead and battle jacket.

It's possible tonight you're on horseback,
The farthest outpost, peering along, with a gun in your fist,
Smiling, whispering, to your exhausted horse.
Maybe—I keep imagining—you are spending the night
As a guest in a strange castle with a park
And writing a letter by candlelight, and tapping
On the piano keys by the window,
Groping for a sound . . .
                              —And maybe
You are already silent, already dead, and the day
Will shine no longer into your beloved
Serious eyes, and your beloved brown hand hangs wilted,
And your white forehead split open——Oh, if only,

Hätt ich dir einmal noch, am letzten Tag,
Hätt ich dir etwas noch gezeigt, gesagt
Von meiner Liebe, die zu schüchtern war!

Du kennst mich ja, du weisst . . . Und lächelnd nickst
Du in die Nacht vor deinem fremden Schloss,
Und nickst auf deinem Pferd im nassen Wald,
Und nickst im Schlaf auf deiner harten Streu,
Und denkst an mich und lächelst.
                              Und vielleicht,
Vielleicht kommst du einmal vom Krieg zurück,
Und eines Abends trittst du bei mir ein,
Man spricht von Longwy, Lüttich, Dammerkirch,
Und lächelt ernst, und alles ist wie einst,
Und keiner sagt ein Wort von seiner Angst,
Von seiner Angst und Zärtlichkeit bei Nacht im Feld,
Von seiner Liebe. Und mit einem Witz
Schreckst du die Angst, den Krieg, die bangen Nächte,
Das Wetterleuchten scheuer Männerfreundschaft
Ins kühle Nie und Nimmermehr zurück.

[1915]

If only, just once, that last day, I had shown you, told you
Something of my love, that was too timid to speak!

But you know me, you know . . . and, smiling, you nod
Tonight in front of your strange castle,
And you nod to your horse in the drenched forest,
And you nod in your sleep to your harsh clutter of straw,
And think about me, and smile.
                                            And maybe,
Maybe some day you will come back from the war,
And take a walk with me some evening,
And somebody will talk about Longwy, Lüttich,
    Dammerkirch,
And smile gravely, and everything will be as before,
And no one will speak a word of his worry,
Of his worry and tenderness by night in the field,
Of his love. And with a single joke
You will frighten away the worry, the war, the uneasy
    nights,
The summer lightning of shy human friendship,
Into the cool past that will never come back.

Herbsttag

(NOVEMBER 1914)

Für Augenblicke schweigt die Ferne mir,
Und alle Berge leuchten
Bläulich herüber aus der feuchten
Novemberluft in junger, weisser Zier.
Die blanken Gipfel stehen,
Wie ich in guter Zeit
Sie oft voll Lust gesehen
Und weit hinunter frisch verschneit.
Kein Mensch ringsum, die Herden sind im Tal,
Verlassene Weiden schweigen winterkahl.

   Auf kühler Rast mess ich die Ferne
   Mit ruhigem Blick, und sehe Abendblau,
   Und ahne hinterm Grat die ersten Sterne,
   Und wittre atmend nahen Reif und Tau—
   Da mit dem Abendschauer
   Kommt mir Erinnerung zurück
   Und Zorn und Leid und tiefe Trauer—
   Ade, mein Wanderglück!

Und wieder stehen meine Gedanken
Zitternd über dem fernen Kampf,
Atmen Brand, atmen Schlachtendampf,
Zittern mit tausend Verwundeten, Sterbenden, Kranken,

Autumn Day

(NOVEMBER 1914)

For moments at a time, the distance is silent,
And all the mountains grow light
Blue overhead, and glow in the moist
November air like young white ornaments.
The hilltops stand bare
As so often, joyfully, I've seen them
In a better time
With fresh snow fallen beneath them.
Not a person around me, the flocks are in the valley,
Abandoned meadows lie still in their winter nakedness.

In a cool resting place, I measure the distance
With a peaceful gaze, and I see the blue of the
evening,
And sense the first star behind the ridge,
And, breathing in, I sense the approaching
Frost and dew. Then, with my evening shiver,
Memory comes back to me
And fury and suffering and deep lamentation—
So much for my joy in wandering.

And again my thoughts stand up
Trembling over the distant struggle,
Inhale gangrene, inhale the reek of the battle,
Tremble with thousands of the wounded, the dying, the
sick,

Suchen mit verirrtem Gefühl
Liebe Brüder im Donner und Schlachtgewühl,
Hängen wie Kinder an guter Mutter Hand
Dankbar und bangend am lieben Vaterland.

[1915]

And search, with blundering feelings,
For beloved brothers in the blasting and tearing of the
    battle,
And cling like children to the hands of their good mother
Grateful and full of anguish for my fatherland.

Den Kindern

(ENDE 1914)

Ihr wisst nichts von der Zeit,
Wisst nur, dass irgendwo im Weiten
Ein Krieg geschlagen wird,
Ihr zimmert Holz zu Schwert und Schild und Speer
Und kämpft im Garten selig euer Spiel,
Schlagt Zelte auf,
Tragt weisse Binden mit dem roten Kreuz.
Und hat mein liebster Wunsch für euch Gewalt,
So bleibt der Krieg
Für euch nur dunkle Sage allezeit,
So steht ihr nie im Feld
Und tötet nie
Und fliehet nie aus brandzerstörtem Haus.

Dennoch sollt ihr einst Krieger sein
Und sollt einst wissen,
Dass dieses Lebens süsser Atem,
Dass dieses Herzschlags liebes Eigentum
Nur Lehen ist, und dass durch euer Blut
Vergangenheit und Ahnenerbe
Und fernste Zukunft rollt,
Und dass für jedes Haar auf eurem Haupt
Ein Kampf, ein Weh, ein Tod erlitten ward.

To Children

(AT THE END OF 1914)

You know nothing of time,
You know only that, somewhere in the distance,
A war is being fought,
You whittle your wood into sword and shield and spear
And play your game blissfully in the garden,
Set up tents,
Carry white bandages marked with the red cross.
And if my wish for you has any power,
So war will remain
For you, always, only a dim legend,
So you will never stand in the field
And never die
And never rush out of a house crumbling in fire.

Nevertheless, you will be soldiers one day
And one day you will know
That the sweet breath of this life,
The precious possession of the heartbeat,
Is only a loan, and that whatever was lost
In the past, and the heir you long for,
And the farthest future,
Rolls through your blood,
And that for every hair on your head
Somebody endured one struggle, one pain, one death.

Und wissen sollt ihr, dass der Edle
In seiner Seele immer Krieger ist,
Auch der nie Waffen trug,
Dass jeden Tag ein Feind,
Dass jeden Tag ein Kampf und Schicksal wartet.
Vergesst es nicht!
Gedenkt des Bluts, der Schlachten, der Zerstörung,
Auf denen eure Zukunft ruht,
Und wie auf Tod und Opfer vieler
Das kleinste Glück sich baut.

Dann werdet ihr das Leben lodernder
Und werdet inniger einst den Tod umarmen.

[1915]

And you shall know that whatever is noble
In your soul is always a warrior,
Even though he bears no weapons,
That every day a struggle and a destiny is waiting.
Do not forget this!
Think of the blood, the shambles, the ruin
On which your own future reposes,
And how, even more, upon death and sacrifice is builded
The tiniest happiness.

Then your life will flame out more
And one day gather even death
Into its arms.

Auch die Blumen

Auch die Blumen leiden den Tod,
Die doch ohne Schuld sind.
So auch ist unser Wesen rein
Und leidet nur Schmerz,
Wo es sich selber nicht mag verstehn.
Was wir Schuld genannt,
Ist von der Sonne aufgesogen,
Kommt längst aus reinen Kelchen der Blumen
Uns entgegen als Duft und rührender Kinderblick.
Und wie die Blumen sterben,
So sterben auch wir
Nur den Tod der Erlösung,
Nur den Tod der Wiedergeburt.

[1911]

Flowers, Too

Flowers, too, suffer death,
And yet they are guiltless.
So, too, our own being is pure
And suffers only grief,
Where we ourselves do not wish to understand.
What we call guilt
Is absorbed by the sun,
It comes to meet us out of the pure throats
Of flowers, fragrance and the moving gaze of children.
And as flowers die,
So we die, too,
Only the death of deliverance,
Only the death of rebirth.

Angst in der Nacht

Die Uhr spricht ängstlich mit dem Spinnweb an der Wand,
Am Laden reisst der Wind,
Meine flackernden Kerzen sind
Ganz vertropft und heruntergebrannt,
Kein Wein im Glase mehr,
Schatten in allen Ecken,
Deren lange Finger sich nach mir strecken.

Wie in der Kinderzeit
Schliess ich die Augen und atme schwer,
Angst hält mich kauernd im Stuhl gefangen.
Aber keine Mutter kommt mehr,
Keine gute, scheltende Magd mehr gegangen,
Die mich am Arm nimmt und mir die schreckliche Welt
Freundlich entzaubert and neu mit Trost erhellt.
Lange bleib ich im Finstern kauern,
Höre den Wind im Dach und den knisternden Tod in den
    Mauern,
Höre Sand hinter Tapeten rinnen,
Höre den Tod mit frierenden Fingern spinnen,
Reisse die Augen auf, will ihn sehen und greifen,
Sehe ins Leere und höre ihn fern
Aus den spöttischen Lippen leise pfeifen,
Taste zum Bett—schliefe, schliefe so gern!
Aber Schlaf ist ein scheuer Vogel geworden,

Uneasiness in the Night

The clock speaks uneasily with the spider web on the wall,
The wind tears at the shutters,
My flickering candles are
Utterly dripped away and burned down,
No more wine in the glass,
Shadows in every corner
Whose long fingers stretch out toward me.

Just as in childhood
I close my eyes and breathe heavily,
Uneasiness clutches me cowering in my chair,
But no mother comes any more,
No kindly, scolding maid comes to me any more
So friendly, she charmed the horrifying world
Away from me and brightened me new with comfort.
I stay a long time, cowering in the darkness,
Hear the wind in the roof and crackling death in the walls,
Hear sand running behind the wallpaper,
Hear death spinning with his cold fingers;
I force my eyes open, I want to look and to grasp,
Look into the emptiness and hear him far off
Whistling lightly out of his mocking lips,
I edge into bed—I wish I could sleep!
But sleep has turned into a frightened bird,

Schwer zu fangen, zu halten, doch leicht zu morden;
Pfeifend fährt er, die Stimme voll bittrem Hohn,
Sausenden Fluges im zerrenden Winde davon.

[1911]

Difficult to catch, to hold, yet easy to kill;
Whistling he flies off, his voice full of bitter disdain,
The rustling of a wing, away in the straining wind.

Alle Tode

Alle Tode bin ich schon gestorben,
Alle Tode will ich wieder sterben,
Sterben den hölzernen Tod im Baum,
Sterben den steinernen Tod im Berg,
Irdenen Tod im Sand,
Blätternen Tod im knisternden Sommergras
Und den armen, blutigen Menschentod.

Blume will ich wieder geboren werden,
Baum und Gras will ich wieder geboren werden,
Fisch und Hirsch, Vogel und Schmetterling.
Und aus jeder Gestalt
Wird mich Sehnsucht reissen die Stufen
Zu den letzten Leiden,
Zu den Leiden des Menschen hinan.

O zitternd gespannter Bogen,
Wenn der Sehnsucht rasende Faust
Beide Pole des Lebens
Zueinander zu biegen verlangt!
Oft noch und oftmals wieder
Wirst du mich jagen von Tod zu Geburt
Der Gestaltungen schmerzvolle Bahn,
Der Gestaltungen herrliche Bahn.

[1921]

All Deaths

I have already died all deaths,
And I am going to die all deaths again,
Die the death of the wood in the tree,
Die the stone death in the mountain,
Earth death in the sand,
Leaf death in the crackling summer grass
And the poor bloody human death.

I will be born again, flowers,
Tree and grass I will be born again,
Fish and deer, bird and butterfly.
And out of every form,
Longing will drag me up the stairways
To the last suffering,
Up to the suffering of men.

O quivering tensed bow,
When the raging fist of longing
Commands both poles of life
To bend to each other!
Yet often, and many times over,
You will hunt me down from death to birth
On the painful track of the creations,
The glorious track of the creations.